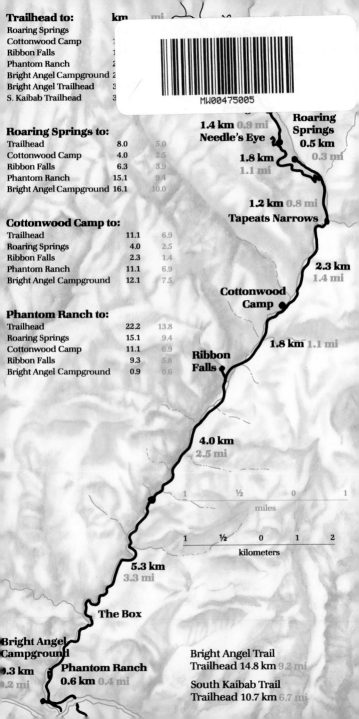

Trailhead to:	km	mi
Roaring Springs		
Cottonwood Camp	1	
Ribbon Falls	1	
Phantom Ranch	2	
Bright Angel Campground	2	
Bright Angel Trailhead	3	
S. Kaibab Trailhead	3	

Roaring Springs to:

	km	mi
Trailhead	8.0	5.0
Cottonwood Camp	4.0	2.5
Ribbon Falls	6.3	3.9
Phantom Ranch	15.1	9.4
Bright Angel Campground	16.1	10.0

Cottonwood Camp to:

	km	mi
Trailhead	11.1	6.9
Roaring Springs	4.0	2.5
Ribbon Falls	2.3	1.4
Phantom Ranch	11.1	6.9
Bright Angel Campground	12.1	7.5

Phantom Ranch to:

	km	mi
Trailhead	22.2	13.8
Roaring Springs	15.1	9.4
Cottonwood Camp	11.1	6.9
Ribbon Falls	9.3	5.8
Bright Angel Campground	0.9	0.6

1.4 km 0.9 mi
Needle's Eye

Roaring Springs
0.5 km 0.3 mi

1.8 km
1.1 mi

1.2 km 0.8 mi
Tapeats Narrows

2.3 km
1.4 mi

Cottonwood Camp

1.8 km 1.1 mi

Ribbon Falls

4.0 km
2.5 mi

1   ½   0   1
miles

1   ½   0   1   2
kilometers

5.3 km
3.3 mi

The Box

Bright Angel Campground

9.3 km
5.2 mi

Phantom Ranch
0.6 km 0.4 mi

Bright Angel Trail
Trailhead 14.8 km 9.2 mi

South Kaibab Trail
Trailhead 10.7 km 6.7 mi

MW00475005

There is a good deal of information available on how to have a minimum impact on the desert while hiking or backpacking. In a very real sense, you are part of the environment that you will pass through—that awareness should be reflected in your actions. *In other words, walk softly—don't scar the desert with cigarette butts or cans and let the flowers continue to grow.* Keep the visible signs of your passing to a minimum.

A Note on the Maps

To develop strip maps for this guide, the North Kaibab Trail was hiked several times using a mileage wheel to come as close as possible on distances. However, the trail is subject to heavy spring runoff and sections require reconstruction almost every spring. Because of this, there may be minor errors in trail placement and distances.

Mule riders on the old Bright Angel Trail. National Park Service photo.

Day Hikes

There are several possibilities for day hikes along the North Kaibab Trail. Remember to carry at least 2 quarts (2 liters) of water per person. During the summer, it is best to hike during the early morning or late afternoon to avoid the hottest part of the day. Day hikers should also carry some food or snacks. Remember that it will probably take you twice as long to hike out of the Canyon as it did to hike in. Popular day hikes on the North Kaibab Trail include (distances and times are for the round trip): Coconino Overlook, 2.2 km (1.4 mi), 1 hour; Supai Tunnel, 5.8 km (3.6 mi), 2½ hours; Redwall Bridge, 8.6 km (5.4 mi), 4 hours; Needle's Eye, 11.2 km (7 mi), 5 hours; Roaring Springs, 16 km (10 mi), 8 hours.

Permits are not required for day hiking in the Canyon, but you do need to obtain them for overnight trips.

History of the Trail

The lure of the Grand Canyon, of penetrating its depths, dates back hundreds of years. Even in prehistoric times, the North Kaibab and Bright Angel trails leading into the Canyon

François Matthes mapping the Grand Canyon. National Park Service photo.

were major access routes. The reason for this early and continued use is that both trails follow the Bright Angel Fault which creates a natural break in the cliffs. While water and a warmer climate in the Inner Canyon were probably responsible for prehistoric travel and occupation along this natural route, later adventurers came in search of minerals and the riches of tourism.

The Anasazi, or "ancient ones," inhabited the area around 1100 A.D., raising crops and building dwellings along Bright Angel Creek and at its delta. Shortly thereafter, however, the area was abandoned by these peoples.

While miners undoubtedly explored the area along the trail, few of their exploits have been recorded. The first documented exploration took place in 1902 when Francois Matthes descended this route from the North Rim with a United States Geological Survey party engaged in mapping the Canyon from Muav Saddle to Bright Angel Point. In an attempt to avoid returning to Bass Camp to the west to make a river crossing, they explored the head of Bright Angel Canyon and came across two miners who were just coming out of the Canyon. With their advice, Matthes descended the trail, crossed the river, and made his way to the South Rim.

Two years later, just as Matthes was completing his map of the area, E. D. Wooley, a prominent Kanab, Utah businessman, formed the Grand Canyon Transportation Company with his son-in-law David Rust. With the help of the other investors, they developed the trail and established a camp close to the Colorado River. They also built a cable car across the river which until this time had to be forded in boats while the livestock swam.

Access to the North Rim itself was difficult and this curtailed the number of people using the North Kaibab Trail. In 1901, the railroad reached the South Rim, bringing increasing numbers of tourists and establishing the more well developed Bright Angel Trail (leading down from the South Rim) as the major tourist route into the Canyon.

With establishment of the national park in 1919, considerable trail work was undertaken. Until this time, the North Kaibab Trail followed Bright Angel Canyon from the rim to the river. When the trail followed this route it was viewed as an extension of the Bright Angel Trail and was known by the same name. In 1926, the National Park Service reconstructed the upper section of the North Rim trail through Roaring Springs Canyon to the west. This new section met the original trail at Manzanita Canyon and the entire trail was given its own name—the North Kaibab Trail. Blasting was done in the lower section of the trail, called the "Box," to avoid some of the 40-odd stream crossings.

During the 1930s the Civilian Conservation Corps continued improvements on the North Kaibab and built the Clear Creek and River trails.

With visitation to Grand Canyon National Park rising yearly, there was a critical shortage of water by the early 1960s, and construction began on a trans-canyon pipeline from Roaring Springs to the South Rim. In 1966, with much of the construction complete, a major flood destroyed the pipeline. Reconstruction began in 1967 and the pipeline was buried under the North Kaibab Trail. Four new foot bridges were built during the project.

In recent years, the number of hikers traveling the cross-canyon corridor (Bright Angel, North and South Kaibab Trails) has increased dramatically and now exceeds 50,000 per year—a marked change from Matthes' small party breaking brush to reach the river.

Geology Along the Trail

The North Kaibab Trail leads you through one of the finest displays of geologic history to be found anywhere. The geologic formations tell an ancient story of when and how the rocks were deposited and formed. These formations range in age from 200 million years old at the rim to two billion years old at the river. Long after the uppermost layer, the Kaibab Limestone, was deposited, the area was uplifted and erosion began cutting the Grand Canyon.

How the Grand Canyon was formed is still a controversial subject and there are several theories. These theories, however, concern themselves with the course of the river and with the descriptions of topographic features. We do know that the Grand Canyon formed somewhere between six and 25 million years ago by different processes of erosion. Water and gravity played a major role by causing mass wasting—landslides, mudflows, talus slides, rock falls, etc. Examples of all these erosional processes are evident along the trail and continue to widen the Grand Canyon.

Gamble oak

Faulting, or the displacement of a continuous body of rock along a place of fracture, has also played a role in the formation of the Grand Canyon. The North Kaibab Trail follows the Roaring Springs and Bright Angel faults both of which resulted from the uplift of the Kaibab Plateau.

Quaking aspen

Ecology of the Trail

The extreme elevational change (and associated precipitation and temperature variations) in the Grand Canyon produce a variety of habitats. The North Rim receives approximately 66 cm (26 in) of precipitation annually, and temperatures range from approximately 12 degrees C. (10 F.) to 26 degreesC.(80 F.). As you descend into the Canyon the climate becomes warmer and drier. The bottom of the Canyon receives only about 15 cm (6 in) of precipitation a year and summer temperatures may reach 48 degrees C. (120 F.).

Five of the seven life zones that C. Hart Merriam divided the North American continent into are found between the North Rim and the Colorado River. Few places on the continent exhibit such diversity in such short a distance—from the Lower Sonoran Zone at 365 m (1200 ft) to the Hudsonian Zone at over 2740 m (9000 ft.). Within each of these zones, communities of plant and animal life have adapted in ways that are unique and form an interesting part of the Grand Canyon story.

All of these diverse habitat types and their associated fauna and flora have one thing in common. Every living system is a complex network of shared energy and resources. As in all ecosystems, interdependence and interaction are essential if the community is to continue.

The Trailhead

At the North Kaibab trailhead you are standing on the Kaibab Plateau which rises approximately 365 m (1200 ft) higher than the South Rim. Before the Grand Canyon was formed, this area was uplifted and stood between 1220 m (4000 ft) and 2440 m (8000 ft) higher than it does today due to additional rock layers that have since eroded. Even today, some 15 cm (6 in) of rock are stripped away from the Kaibab Plateau every thousand years.

You are now standing on the Kaibab Limestone, the uppermost of the rock formations in the Grand Canyon. This formation was deposited about 200 million years ago when this area was covered with a shallow, warm water sea which supported a varied population of marine organisms including corals, sponges and sharks. Fossils of these organisms can be seen as you hike along the trail.

The word "Kaibab" means "mountain lying down" in the language of the Southern Paiute Indians and at one time this plateau

Mule deer

was called Buckskin Mountain by hunters and trappers because of the abundance of deer. This island in the surrounding desert supports a variety of fauna and flora; mule deer (*Odocoileus hemionus*), and coyotes (*Canis lupus*) are common sights. Dominant forest vegetation includes the ponderosa pine (*Pinus ponderosa*), white fir (*Abies concolor*), and the quaking aspen (*Populus tremuloides*). The Kaibab is spotted with expansive meadows containing numerous species of wildflowers.

The slope-forming Toroweap Formation overlies the buff-colored Coconino Sandstone cliff.

(opposite) Ancient reptile tracks fossilized in Coconino Sandstone. It is rare to find these fossils along the trail today because many have been removed illegally by collectors. National Park Service photo.

Coconino Overlook

From this point at the top of the Coconino Sandstone, you are looking down Roaring Springs Canyon to its intersection with Bright Angel Canyon coming in from the northeast. The South Rim may be seen across the Canyon and on clear days you can see the San Francisco Peaks rise above the horizon over 112 km (70 mi) away. Flagstaff, Arizona is located at the base of the mountains.

You are standing at the base of the Toroweap Formation deposited by an inland sea some 230 million years ago. As this sea advanced it covered already existing sand dunes with sea muds, sands, and limes. These sea deposits formed the Toroweap Formation, and the underlying dune sands were cemented together forming the vertical buff-colored cliffs of the Coconino Formation below. A close inspection of the Coconino reveals cross-bedding caused by wind shifting these dunes some 240 million years ago. The desert environment at that time supported reptiles and scorpions whose tracks have been found fossilized in this sandstone.

The slopes below the North Rim support a variety of plants. Small changes in precipitation, temperature, exposure and soil depth can create very different habitats. Where sunlight is limited and the soil deep, trees such as fir, aspen and Gambel oak (*Quercus gambelii*) can be common. Where soil is limited and exposure direct, dry-tolerant species like pinyon and juniper are found. At this elevation you are in a transitional zone between vegetational species.

Supai Tunnel

This tunnel was blasted through the Supai group during the 1930s when this section of the North Kaibab Trail was built to replace the old Bright Angel Trail to the northeast.

The Supai group, and the Hermit Shale above it, were formed about 260 million years ago when this was a predominantly swampy area which supported ferns, conifers and numerous amphibians and reptiles.

Rock layers in the Grand Canyon and elsewhere vary in hardness and thus vary in resistance to erosion. Hard layers of rock form vertical cliffs while softer layers form slopes and terraces. The harder layers, including limestone and sandstone, are made up of relatively large rock particles. Sandstone particles are cemented with calcite or silica. The buff-colored Coconino and the red Supai

Ponderosa pine roots

group are good examples of more resistant rock. Limestone, a chemical precipitate of calcium carbonate, is also erosion resistant. The Kaibab Limestone at the rim, and the Redwall Limestone below, exemplify cliff-forming layers. Rock layers which are relatively softer, like shale, are composed of fine-grained minerals with little cementing material between the grains. These less resistant rocks are more easily broken apart and eroded away. The slope-forming Toroweap and Hermit formations above are good examples of this principle.

Around this tunnel in the Supai and the environs below, you are in the pinyon pine *(Pinus edulis)* and Utah juniper *(Juniperus osteosperma)* forest. Already, water is more limited than at higher elevations and Douglas and white firs can only survive in small, protected microclimates. Here also you find shrubs that are associated with the pinyon-juniper woodland; cliffrose *(Cowania mexicana)*, broadleaf yucca *(Yucca baccata)*, serviceberry *(Amelanchier utahensis)*, and rabbitbrush *(Chrysothamnus nauseosus)*.

These species have been able to adapt to a transitional climate zone that can receive accumulations of snow in the winter and be hot and dry during the summer months. The cool moist forests above are left behind and the vegetation now begins to reflect a desert environment.

The Bridge in the Redwall

The construction of this bridge took place after a major flood in 1966 wiped out much of the North Kaibab Trail. The flood occurred when more than 38 cm (15 in) of rain fell on the North Rim in a 36-hour period. Traces of the old trail can still be seen on the far slope up the drainage.

Floods such as the one that occurred in 1966 are a major force in widening the Grand Canyon. Processes of weathering—cracking from temperature changes, ice or tree roots expanding in rock cracks, wind—occur constantly. Only floods, however, can remove debris that falls from cliffs and slopes into the

The view from Redwall Bridge, looking down a small canyon along the Roaring Springs Fault.

drainage bottoms. For millions of years floods have periodically scoured the bottoms of these side canyons. Here, flood waters follow the Roaring Springs Fault, a zone of shearing which occurred during the uplift of the Kaibab Plateau. Each time a flood comes through, the streambed is cut deeper and the head of the drainage cuts further back into the rim of Roaring Springs Canyon.

Notice the two ponderosa pine trees growing in the drainage below the bridge. They are growing nearly 300 m (1000 ft) below their range. Life zones or ecosystems in which plants can exist are not rigid. Seeds can be dispersed over a wide area by animals and the elements, and they will germinate and take hold if the plant's minimum requirements are met. If a plant or animal successfully lives under minimal conditions, it is said to be in a "marginal" habitat.

Spotted skunk. Illustration by Scott Hecker.

The Eye of the Needle

This dramatic section of the trail, opposite a large spire sometimes called the "Needle," was blasted through the sheer Redwall Limestone. Until recently, the trail passed through a small tunnel called the Needle's Eye which has since broken away from the rock wall. The trail at this point is directly on the Roaring Springs Fault. You'll notice that corresponding rock layers to the east have dropped nearly 55 m (180 ft) below those to the west. This faulting, or displacement of rock strata, took place long before the Canyon was cut. The imposing, sheer cliffs of the Redwall present one of the major barriers in terms of traveling in the Canyon. Without faults which create a natural route through cliff-forming layers like the Redwall, travel would be impossible not only for man, but also for numerous animal species.

Prominent pinnacle of Redwall Limestone.

The Redwall Formation was deposited more than 300 million years ago when a Mississippian Sea covered this area. This sea teemed with life; along with billions of microscopic creatures, there were also corals, nautiloids (similar to the present-day chambered nautilus), and brachiopods (shelled marine animals). When these organisms died, their remains collected on the ocean floor along with calcium carbonate that precipitated out of the water. The land continued to sink as this limey sediment built up. The weight of overlying sediments eventually turned this sediment into limestone. (Because most limestones are formed in a similar manner, marine fossils are common.)

(on the following pages) Roaring Springs

(opposite) Brachiopod and pelecypod fossils illustrate that a sea once covered what is now Grand Canyon. National Park Service photo.

Roaring Springs

Roaring Springs has been the source of water for the North Rim since 1928. In that year, the Union Pacific Railway dammed Bright Angel Creek below the confluence of Bright Angel Creek and Roaring Springs. A penstock carried water downstream to generators located in a powerhouse near the site of the current Roaring Springs residence. This powerhouse generated electricity for facilities on the North Rim and for a pumphouse located at the base of Roaring Springs which supplied the North Rim's water.

In 1979 a new pumphouse was completed which lifts water over 1090 vertical meters (3600 ft) to the North Rim. Since 1970, when a trans-canyon pipeline was completed, Roaring Springs has also been the source of water for the South Rim. The pressure of water in this line carries it to the Colorado River and then to Indian Gardens where it is pumped to the South Rim.

Cattails

Where does the water from Roaring Springs originate? Rain and snowmelt seep into the ground on the North Rim and percolate down through rock strata until the water reaches an impervious layer—in this case, the Muav Limestone. Here it forms a water-table where it is slowly collected and drained through caverns leading to Roaring Springs. This same process takes place along the entire north side of the Canyon, giving birth to numerous springs and waterfalls. Groundwater is an important life-giving resource which responds slowly to climatic fluctuations so that even during dry periods water continues to flow from these springs.

Three different rock strata visible in this area record another time when the land here was covered by inland seas: the brown cliffs of the Tapeats Sandstone, the rolling hills of the grey-green Bright Angel Shale which form the Tonto Plateau, and the buff-colored Muav Limestone which slopes up from the plateau. Together, these formations are called the Tonto Group. About 550 million years ago, a Cambrian sea covered this area and marine life underwent an incredible increase in diversity and density. Multi-cellular animals, which first appeared on the earth earlier, developed into complex algae, sea worms, brachiopods, and vertebrates. Trilobites, a marine arthropod, developed and would continue to thrive in shallow marine environments for the next 250 million years.

(opposite) Ranger Harold Miller displays his catch of trout from Bright Angel Creek, circa 1940. National Park Service photo.

At the bottom of the Redwall, the ecosystem changes dramatically. Trees are limited to washed or shaded slopes, while cacti and shrubs begin to dominate the more open landscape. One of the major adaptations that plants have made to these arid conditions is a reduced leaf surface that conserves water that might be lost through evaporation. In fact, cacti and green-stemmed Mormon tea *(Ephedra viridis)* have no true leaves.

A fish hatchery was operated at the powerhouse in the 1930s and rainbow trout were introduced into Bright Angel Creek. This exotic (non-native) species successfully adapted to this habitat and today can be found along most of Bright Angel Creek. In the late fall they swim upstream from the Colorado River to spawn. Fishing is permitted with a valid Arizona fishing license.

Kingfisher. Illustration by Scott Hecker.

The Tapeats Narrows

Below this narrow canyon through the Tapeats Sandstone you can see huge piles of alluvium, or muds, sands, and rock that have been deposited by running water. These deposits are the remains of older stream beds when the creek followed a different course and before it cut down to its current level. You can also see further evidence of erosion—large slump blocks of Tapeats Sandstone have sheared off and fallen to the slopes below, eventually to be broken up and carried to the Colorado River and toward the Gulf of California.

Tapeats Narrows frame Deva Temple.

On the section of the trail below the Tapeats, you traverse the red-colored Dox Sandstone, the uppermost in a series of tilted rock layers which form the Grand Canyon Supergroup. This series of rocks was deposited by seas, swamps and rivers approximately 0.7 to 1.3 billion years ago. After deposition, but still before the Tapeats formed, these layers were faulted and tilted up to the northeast. Mountains were formed and slowly eroded away. In much of the Grand Canyon area, the Grand Canyon Supergroup rocks were completely eroded away before the Tapeats was deposited, and these layers are missing altogether. This geologic contact was named the Great Unconformity by John Wesley Powell, the first scientist to describe the Grand Canyon's geology.

Bright Angel Creek gives life to a lush riparian, or streamside, community which exists in marked contrast to the surrounding desert. In the stream itself, algae, horsetails *(Equisetum spp.)*, cattails *(Typha spp.)*, and various reeds are found. Cottonwoods and willows are also dominant. Vegetation adds oxygen to the water and provides food and shelter for numerous species of birds, insects and amphibians. Deer and other water-dependent mammals use the riparian zone as a passageway into otherwise impenetrable desert areas. A common species of bird along the creek is the dipper *(Cinclus mexicanus)*, a medium size, grey bird with a short tail. It gets its name from its bobbing motion.

Cottonwood Camp

Cottonwood Camp was probably first
established in the 1920s as a layover or
stopping point for mule tours coming down
from the North Rim. It was further developed
by the Civilian Conservation Corps during the
1930s. A ranger station and campground are
located here today and water and restrooms
are available.

The history of human occupation in this area
began long before miners and mule riders.
Over 800 years ago, prehistoric Anasazi Indians
settled along Bright Angel Creek. Hunting
various game animals and gathering edible
wild plants was undertaken, but by 1050 A.D.
agriculture was becoming increasingly
important. The dry farming of corn, beans and
squash took place along the creek and
constituted a major part of their economy.
Once these crops had been harvested, some
were stored in granaries (usually built into
rock ledges) along with water and other foods.
Numerous prehistoric sites and associated
artifacts are located throughout Bright Angel
Canyon. It is important to remember that these
sites and artifacts are protected by law.
Removing or disturbing these remains takes
them out of context and makes it impossible
for archeologists to piece together the culture
of these ancient peoples.

Perhaps the most striking feature of the camp
is the Fremont cottonwoods (*Populus
fremontii*). Fast-growing, water-dependent

trees that are common in riparian habitats throughout the Southwest, they are a welcome sight for hikers just as they must have been for the early pioneers in the region. They provide shade from the sun and also indicate that water is nearby. These trees regulate their own temperature by transpiring copious amounts of water. One large cottonwood can release over 190 liters (50 gal) of water into the air each day.

Cottonwood Camp

(opposite) Campsites under the shade of towering cotton- woods at Cottonwood Campground pro- vide a respite for weary hikers. National Park Service photo.

Between Cottonwood and Wall Creek

The trail below Cottonwood goes over a rise from which you get a good view of the South Rim; Oza Butte looms above to the northwest.

All of the geologic formations on the trail above this point are sedimentary, formed through the accumulation and solidification of sediments. After the red-colored Dox Sandstone (which you see around you) was deposited, igneous (molten) rock was intruded from great depths in the earth. Where this liquid rock crosscut existing rock formations, it formed dikes; where it squeezed in parallel to existing formations, it formed sills. Along this section of the trail you can see intrusive sills in both the Dox and Hakatai formations.

Once you leave the riparian habitat, you will encounter typical desert vegetation. The climate here is hot, and annual precipitation measures less than 25 cm (10 in). Water, the most precious resource here, must be conserved by any species that is to survive. Cacti, narrow-leaf yucca *(Yucca augustissima)*, and Utah agave *(Agave utahensis)* are among the dominant plants and are highly successful at maintaining their internal moisture. Adaptations like succulent tissues to hold moisture, waxy coatings on leaves to decrease evaporation, and growing close to the ground to minimize exposure to the wind, are necessary in this arid environment. Many species have developed spines to protect them from foraging animals, but also to decrease the amount of water lost through transpiration. One of the most widespread desert trees, mesquite *(Prosopis juliflora)*, grows about 4 m (15 ft) tall and is abundant in this area. This desert plant has adapted to a dry environment by sending roots down as far as 15 m (50 ft).

Ribbon Falls

Ribbon Falls can be reached by taking a short hike off the main trail. Cross the bridge and follow the trail to the southwest and then proceed by a small side canyon. Return to the main trail by this same route, as crossing the stream is hazardous and could easily result in a broken leg or arm.

Mule riders during the 1930s view Ribbon Falls. Today, no camping is allowed in this area. National Park Service photo.

The waters of Ribbon Creek flow through limestone formations above, dissolving and carrying calcium carbonate in solution. This calcium carbonate, or lime, precipitates out of solution at the fall and forms a rock called

travertine. The large, moss-covered apron below the fall is formed of this travertine.

The species of vegetation you find at Ribbon Falls are obviously quite different than those found in the surrounding desert. Mosses, maidenhair fern *(Adiantum Capillus-veniris)*, yellow columbine *(Aquilegia chrysantha)*, and monkeyflower *(Mimulus spp.)* are delicate water-loving plants which thrive in the microclimate created by Ribbon Falls.

Protect this fragile environment. No camping, no fires. Scars can take years to heal.

The Box

At the northern end of The Box you stand at the geologic contact between the Bass Formation and the Vishnu Group. The Bass Formation represents the oldest sedimentary rock layer in the Canyon. The Vishnu Schist is metamorphic. Metamorphic rocks are igneous or sedimentary rocks that have been transformed by heat and pressure. The contact between these formations represents a tremendous gap in time during which the Vishnu rocks were deposited, a mountain range was formed, then eroded away, and the Bass Formation was deposited.

The Bass Formation was deposited about a billion years ago when this area was covered alternately by a shallow sea and mud flats. This formation contains the earliest record of plant life found in the Grand Canyon. Fossils of algae in thin horizontal layers called stromatolites are often found in this layer. These algae were not significantly different than the algae found in Bright Angel Creek today.

Vertical walls of schist rise 360 m (1200 ft) above you in The Box. These rocks are approximately two billion years old. A thick sequence of sediments and lavas covered the land long before any of the rock found here today was formed. About 1.7 billion years ago a period of great compression occurred causing these sediments to buckle and fold. Mountains that could have been as high as today's Himalayas were created while other rocks were pushed far into the earth's crust and under tremendous heat and pressure were metamorphosed.

(opposite) This exposed pipeline was once buried under the North Kaibab Trail in The Box, two and a half miles above Phantom Ranch. Flood waters destroyed this portion of the trail in 1995. National Park Service photo.

Collared lizard. Illustration by Scott Hecker.

After these mountains were formed, they were slowly worn down by erosion. Later uplifts occurred and the overlying rock layers were stripped away, revealing metamorphic rocks that were formed 8 km (5 mi) below the earth's surface.

Along the entire North Kaibab Trail you will be struck by the diversity of life forms and the contrast between the lush riparian zone along Bright Angel Creek and the aridity of the desert environment. In The Box this contrast is even sharper because of their closeness to each other. Along the creek, box elder (*Acer negundo*) grows along with a variety of grasses and sedges. Look for numerous species of birds and listen for the descending call of the canyon wren (*Catherpes mexicanus*).

A short distance from the creek a few desert-tolerant plant species exist and even venture to live on the vertical walls themselves. Chuckwallas (*Sauromalus obesus*), desert collared lizards (*Crotaphytas collaris*), and other desert reptiles like the Grand Canyon rattlesnake (*Crotalis viridis abyssus*) can also be found here.

Phantom Ranch

In 1869 Major John Wesley Powell led the first scientific expedition through the Grand Canyon on the Colorado River. During their traverse they stopped on the delta where Bright Angel Creek enters the Colorado, and Powell named the tributary "Silver Creek." Later, when writing popular accounts of the journey, he changed the name to Bright Angel. Powell, however, may not have been the first white man to see the creek. Perhaps the first visitor was a barely literate prospector who came completely by accident.

One of the early bridges over Bright Angel Creek. National Park Service photo.

Two years before Powell made his traverse, James White and several companions were ambushed by Indians along the Colorado or one of its tributaries north of the Grand Canyon. White's companions were killed and in order to escape he built a raft and took to the river. Fourteen days later, he was pulled from the

river (half-starved and nearly dead) at Callville below the Grand Canyon. Even today, a minor controversy rages as to whether White actually made the trip, and there is some speculation that he may have invented the story to cover a murder. However, he may have been the first Anglo to float through the Canyon and the first to see Bright Angel Creek entering from the north.

Phantom Creek

David Rust established the first tourist camp here in 1907. The name Rust's Camp remained until 1913 when President Theodore Roosevelt stayed here on his way to the North Rim with an expedition hunting mountain lions. The

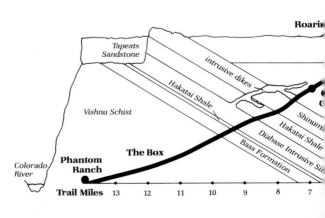

Roari

Tapeats Sandstone

intrusive dikes

Hakatai Shale

Vishnu Schist

Shinum

Hakatai Shale

Diabase Intrusive Si

Bass Formation

The Box

Colorado River

Phantom Ranch

Trail Miles 13   12   11   10   9   8   7